My Little Golden Book About the 90s

By Jennifer Dussling • Illustrated by Spencer Wilson

A GOLDEN BOOK • NEW YORK
Golden Books
An imprint of Random House Children's Books
A division of Penguin Random House LLC
1745 Broadway, New York, NY 10019
penguinrandomhouse.com
rhcbooks.com

Library of Congress Control Number: 2025934104
ISBN 979-8-217-11660-7 (trade) — ISBN 979-8-217-11661-4 (ebook)
Manufactured in the United States of America
10 9 8 7 6 5 4 3 2 1
EU Contact: Penguin Random House Ireland, 32 Nassau Street, Dublin D02 YH68.
https://eu-contact.penguin.ie

What an extraordinary time! The 1990s were the last decade of the twentieth century and the last decade of the millennium. It took 990 years to get there—of course it was going to be a party!

The 1990s were so cool that people found loads of ways to say "cool." Check out what made it so . . .

Nothing screams the '90s like **grunge**. In 1991, grunge music burst out of Seattle, Washington, when Nirvana, led by Kurt Cobain, released the best-selling album *Nevermind*. A mix of rock and punk, grunge was loud and gritty. Nirvana and other grunge bands, like Pearl Jam and Stone Temple Pilots, launched a sound—and a style—that spanned the decade.

The Grunge Look

Not feeling the grunge? Just turn the radio dial to listen to dreamy boy bands, like Boyz II Men, Backstreet Boys, and NSYNC, and the best-selling girl group of all time, the Spice Girls!

Who else made the ’90s hop and bop?

Mariah Carey • Red Hot Chili Peppers
Wu-Tang Clan • Dr. Dre • Radiohead
TLC • Britney Spears • Ricky Martin

One song was heard everywhere in the mid-’90s, from ballparks to weddings to street parties. Partly in English, partly in Spanish, “**Macarena**” came with its own easy-to-learn dance. Hold out one hand, then the other, turn palms up one at a time, shake hips, jump a quarter turn—hey, Macarena!

Food was fun in the '90s. Parents sent kids to school with **Lunchables**—crackers, cheese squares, and ham circles packed in separate little compartments. Kids sipped **Capri Sun** from pouches or gulped down **Sunny D**. Fruit was smashed and rolled thin as fruit leather or roll-ups.

Even restaurants were entertaining! At the **Rainforest Cafe**, which opened in 1994 at the Mall of America, huge fake plants, fog machines, bird calls, and "thunderstorms" made eating out an adventure.

Another adventure? **Rollerblading**! Adults and kids everywhere were zipping around on dope skates with all four wheels lined up in a row. Rollerblades, also called in-line skates, could be tricky to master, though. Good balance—and knee pads, elbow pads, helmets, and wrist guards—definitely helped!

Small toys hit it big with '90s kids. Nine floppy, colorful, pellet-filled stuffed animals appeared on store shelves in 1994. Made by Ty Inc., **Beanie Babies** had names like Splash the Whale, Squealer the Pig, and Patti the Platypus. By the following year, these five-dollar cuties had kicked off an epic toy craze.

As Ty added piles of new styles, some older and rare Beanie Babies—in mint condition and with the original heart-shaped tag—resold for thousands of dollars. Adults started to collect them, hoping to get rich.

Before the decade ended, the Beanie Baby bubble burst. Not everyone minded. Kids were happy to be allowed to play with their toys again. Cool beans!

There were plenty of other tiny toys to play with.

Polly Pocket playsets were small enough to fit in your pocket and had entire miniature worlds inside, with dolls, furniture, pets, and more.

Another mini toy craze? **Tamagotchi**. These virtual pets hatched from a digital egg. Pressing buttons to walk them, play with them, and feed them kept the pets happy and alive—but not forever. Tamagotchi owners learned a hard lesson in pet care when a different egg appeared, and they had to start all over with a new pet.

Kids flipped for **Pogs**! These small, round cardboard discs with a picture on one side were inspired by a game (also called Pogs) that started in Hawaii in the 1930s. Want to play? Mix together your Pogs and your friends' Pogs and stack them with the picture side up. Then take turns hitting the stack with a heavier disc called a slammer. All the Pogs that land with their picture down are now yours!

Sure, the music was great and the toys awesome, but one thing set the 1990s apart from every decade before—the **internet**! Can you even imagine life without it? With just a computer, a modem, and a telephone line, people could dial up and connect to a vast network of information on the **World Wide Web**.

The internet caught on lightning fast. By 1999, 150 million people around the globe used it to read news, buy books, sell things they no longer wanted, and send messages to their friends—hello, email!

The internet wasn't the only big leap forward. In 1997, Scottish scientists broke the news that they had successfully cloned an adult mammal! They took a single cell from an adult sheep and used it to make a baby lamb with the exact same genes. The lamb, named **Dolly**, after Dolly Parton, became the world's most famous sheep.

Clones popped up in movie theaters, too. The 1993 blockbuster **Jurassic Park** imagined an island theme park filled with dinosaurs brought back from extinction by cloning bits of their DNA. The special effects were eye-popping, and the box office sales jaw-dropping. *Jurassic Park* made over 900 million dollars during its original run!

More Cool '90s Movies

Home Alone (1990)
A League of Their Own (1992)
Groundhog Day (1993)
The Lion King (1994)
Forrest Gump (1994)
Toy Story (1995)
Clueless (1995)
Babe (1995)
Titanic (1997)
The Matrix (1999)

Athletes also put on a great show!

The biggest story at the 1992 Barcelona Olympics was USA's Dream Team. Led by **Magic Johnson**, **Larry Bird**, and **Michael Jordan**, this supergroup of legendary pro basketball players easily took home Olympic gold.

In the summer of 1995, athletes at the first **Extreme Games** (renamed X Games in '96) competed in sports not seen at the Olympics like bungee jumping, skysurfing, and skateboarding. Cowabunga!

Even golf became cool, when a phenomenal young player named **Tiger Woods** turned pro in 1996. He won golf's biggest event, the Masters Tournament, the very next year, at just twenty-one years old! Following Tiger's lead, more than 3 million people took up the sport in the '90s.

Topping off the decade, in 1999, the US Women's soccer team won the World Cup on home turf, making stars of **Mia Hamm** and **Brandi Chastain**.

The 1994 fall TV season gave America a bunch of new besties on **Friends**. Clever writing and talented actors made the sitcom a hit almost right away. Viewers loved getting to know Rachel, Monica, Joey, Chandler, Phoebe, and Ross. The show even launched a hair trend—the Rachel. The haircut worn by the character played by Jennifer Aniston was requested at beauty salons across the country. *Friends* ran for ten seasons.

More Cool '90s TV

Full House
Beverly Hills, 90210
Rugrats
Home Improvement
The X-Files
Boy Meets World
Mighty Morphin Power Rangers

"Quirky" is the word to describe lots of '90s TV. The hit show ***Seinfeld*** was famously "about nothing." A cartoon for grown-ups called ***The Simpsons*** became the longest running sitcom ever. The Carlton dance on ***The Fresh Prince of Bel-Air***, the Log Lady on ***Twin Peaks***, and everything about ***Teletubbies*** had audiences saying, "It's weird, but I love it!"

The line between TV and reality blurred in 1992. MTV's new show *The Real World* brought seven strangers to live together in a New York City apartment—and left the cameras on, all day, all night.

Welcome to reality TV! Viewers were hooked. Every week, they tuned in to see what happened "when people stop being polite . . . and start getting real."

As the decade wound down, excitement took hold. What would a new century bring?

Then tech companies sounded an alarm: When we made all those fancy new computers, we forgot to plan for a year that didn't start with "nineteen." On New Year's Day, computers might think it's 1900, not 2000!

The problem was called **Y2K**, shorthand for the year 2000. People around the world panicked. Would planes fall from the sky? Would banks fail? Would the power go out? Some people stockpiled food or built underground bunkers to prepare for Y2K.

On New Year's Eve, everyone held their breath as the countdown started.

10, 9, 8, 7, 6, 5, 4, 3, 2 . . .

. . . 1!

PHEW! Nothing out of the ordinary happened. Planes kept flying, the power stayed on, and the world didn't end. Happy New Year indeed!

What a decade! From cool bands to cool shows, to cool foods and cool clothes, the **'90s** were the jam! Catch you on the flip side. Let's bounce!